**SECOND EDITION:** 30/07/2019
**TITLE:** DISTRIBUTED LIQUIDITY
**SUBTITLE:** HOW GAME THEORY APPLIED TO HELICOPTER MONEY CAN SOLVE EURO CRISIS
**AUTHOR:** ALESSANDRO NOSEI
**LANGUAGE:** ENGLISH
**PUBLISHER:** INDEPENDENTLY PUBLISHED
**ISBN:** 9781073656677
**EDITORIAL MANAGER:** LUCA MARTINO
**TRANSLATION:** CLARE TAME
**COVER:** GESTA.CC

**FIRST EDITION:** 27/07/2016
**TITLE:** LIQUIDITÀ DISTRIBUITA
**SUBTITLE:** UNA SOLUZIONE MONETARIA PER IL BILANCIAMENTO DI SISTEMI ECONOMICI ASIMMETRICI
**AUTHOR:** ALESSANDRO NOSEI
**LANGUAGE:** ITALIAN
**PUBLISHER:** EDIZIONI ITALIA
ISBN: 9788899698003
**EDITORIAL MANAGER:** LUCA MARTINO
**COVER:** GESTA.CC

**TRANSLATOR'S NOTES**

To respect the mathematical formulas, reference was made to the acronyms of the first publication, in Italian. In particular as regards the Monetary Stimulus, we used SM (Stimolo Monetario, in Italian) instead of MS and about the Total Monetary Stimulus, we used SMT (Stimolo Monetario Totale), instead of TMS.

# DISTRIBUTED LIQUIDITY

## How Game Theory applied to Helicopter Money can solve Euro crisis

*Alessandro Nosei*

# CONTENTS

## FORWARD
The Aim of the Essay ............................................................. 5
The Current European Monetary System, Unsustainable Long-term ............ 6
Modelling the Policies of Monetary Stimulus .................................... 13

## DISTRIBUTED LIQUIDITY (DL)
The Objectives of Economic-monetary Politics ................................. 20
Concepts underlying the Distributed Liquidity Model .......................... 21
Automatic Attribution Mechanisms of the Distributed Liquidity Model ....... 23
Definitions ......................................................................... 26
Quantification of the Monetary Stimulus ....................................... 27
Allocation of Monetary Stimulus ................................................ 30
Use of Rewards .................................................................... 32
Self-balancing of the DL Model Long-term ..................................... 34
Creation of Monetary Stimulus .................................................. 39

## EFFECTS OF THE APPLICATION OF THE DL MODEL
Expected Behavior of Agents of Change: Citizens .............................. 43
Expected Behavior of Agents of Change: Businesses ........................... 45
Effects on the Economic System ................................................. 48
Effects on Eurozone National Governments .................................... 50
European Government and the European Central Bank ....................... 55
Macroeconomic and Monetary Effects ........................................... 56

## CONCLUSIONS
Ethical Considerations in Applying the DL Model .............................. 60

## ADDENDUM
New Fields of Research ........................................................... 63
Simulation of the Distributed Liquidity Model .................................. 65

## BIBLIOGRAPHY ............................................................... 67

# FORWARD

## The Aim of the Essay

This essay will illustrate a new model of monetary policy with the aim of solving the economic problems and imbalances currently affecting European countries. In the discussion we will show that it is possible to do the following:

1. Permanently reduce the public debt of the most backward countries

2. Reduce the differences in per capita income among the citizens of the various European countries

3. Relaunch the economies of the least performing countries in a structural way

4. Enhance the capacities of the best performing countries, offering even more development prospects

5. Balance the inflationary pressures between countries by nourishing deflationary forces in countries in recession

6. Create a system that tends to the cohesion of countries, instead of their separation

7. Make the European market the best performing market globally in the long term

8. Accomplish all this by making the free market work and not using assistance logics.

To obtain these results, an unconventional model for the use of money will be proposed; We are convinced that in the face of new challenges, such as the creation of a single currency in a System of Confederate countries, it is necessary to adopt new instruments to manage economic imbalances.

# THE CURRENT EUROPEAN MONETARY SYSTEM AND ITS LONG-TERM UNSUSTAINABILITY

## THE EUROPEAN MONETARY SYSTEM AS AN IMPERFECT AND INCOMPLETE SYSTEM

In recent years the Community project, inspired by universally shared values, has suffered a serious setback as a result of economic crisis and geopolitical pressure; the European Single Market and the Single European Currency were not followed up by political and fiscal union.

Monetary union has been applied to Eurozone countries with very different economic models and productive "speeds". On the positive side, this has created greater transparency, facilitated exchange, helps cover for financial risk and means lower operational costs for business. On the negative side, the end of national exchange rates has introduced a very strong element of rigidity in automatic market adjustment. This element alone has turned out to be a driver of economic depression for the entire Eurozone system and has had a greater impact than the benefits listed above.

The result highlights the fact that economic and monetary systems based on the noble values of solidarity and altruism do not function when strongly negative economic conditions subject citizens, businesses, and thus governments, to pressure. Without the right sort of model the search for individual national interest will inevitably re-emerge and feed forms of anti-Communitarian populism together with protectionist tendencies that exploit the economic crisis and the misgivings of citizens and businesses alike.

The study presents a mechanism to maintain Europe's current monetary and economic union, with all its far-reaching and indisputable benefits, whilst freeing up untapped economic potential blocked by market rigidity.

## Heterogeneous Productivity in the Eurozone is at the Root of the Problem in EU Countries

National economic performance is shaped by many factors but can be summed up in 4 basic points:

- **Market size and economies of scale.** Being able to count on an internal market which is so much larger than any individual Member State allows for strong economies of scale, and hence a greater level of systemic efficiency. This factor is a given value and operates independent of governments' policies. Yet, in outlining a sustainable economic model we must pursue the goal of extending equity to countries that do not have the opportunity to compete in terms of size.

- **Cultural factors, training, skills and human capital.** These are arguably the most important drivers of economic growth. The ability to organize business efficiently depends on human capital, particularly businessmen, entrepreneurs and managers of public and private economic structures.

- **Rules, regulations, bureaucracy and economic policy.** These are the result of the previous point (in the public sector) and more resistant to change over time. The regulatory and normative framework is a driver with a determining impact on economic growth which it either inhibits or facilitates.

- **Taxation.** This has a direct impact on attracting foreign capital and business and hence on acquiring resources from outside the national system. It also has a direct impact on the supply and demand mechanism for goods and services.

The European Union faces enormous disparities in economic performance among its Eurozone members, due to the marked heterogeneity of these drivers, together with other factors.

## An 'Imperfect Structure': Exchange Rates as an Automatic Adjustment Mechanism

In a complex system where culturally diverse management models for the state and business create different levels of competition and economic performance, the main mechanism to regulate markets and capital is the adjustment of the real value of goods and services through national exchange rates.

If a country has the capacity to create lower value added than another country and maintains its standard of living over time (pensions, public-sector wages, advantageous rentier positions, etc.), we will inevitably see an increase in indebtedness. The exchange rate will progressively devalue the national currency until exports become competitive again and direct investment in the country will become so advantageous that foreign firms will be persuaded to relocate parts of their productive system in order to obtain economic advantages in operational costs.

The end of national currencies in the Eurozone has inhibited this process, on the assumption that the simple adjustment of supply and demand in a free market and the growth of single Member States in the medium to long term will offset this shortcoming by balancing out markets.

Furthermore, the national central banks' loss of monetary management autonomy, has inhibited the capability of acting with monetary policies to balance national economies.

In actual fact, Member States, without the exchange rate mechanism and the traditional tools of monetary policy, may act only with economic domestic policies and eventual lack of competitivity and lack of capacity to carry out structural reforms will finally result with extra deficit and hence indebtedness.

The defect of this framework is that if a government is not strong enough to carry out structural reform it will be trapped in a vicious circle of increasing debt, but without the safety net of monetary devaluation.

In this scenario it is difficult to exit this downward spiral and this is why there is a strong risk that a EU member state may want to leave the monetary system to avoid national default.

## Inhibitors of Automatic Adjustment Mechanisms for Supply & Demand in the Monetary System

Liberal purists claim that in the long run where there are blocked exchange rates markets can adjust automatically via prices. The entire Euro currency project has been based on this assumption. Yet this is only partially true since some variables do not follow (or only at a very high economic cost) demand/supply adjustment. These are the main ones:

- **Downward wage rigidities.** Lower productivity should follow lower wages. But wages have extremely rigid downward adjustment dynamics. If workers accept, albeit unwillingly, a reduction of real purchasing power through a wage freeze and moderate (i.e. less perceptible) inflation, direct cuts in public and private sector wages will be politically unacceptable, given the risk of acute social tensions and pressure making it unsustainable and unworkable for any democratic government. Furthermore, acting on this lever will create an economic shock in demand and thus a further recessionary downward spiral.

- **Inelastic prices when responding to downward price trends for basic goods.** In general, even if more elastic than wages, the price of basic goods has a more rigid downward mechanism compared to the mechanism for price rises. Furthermore, business could benefit from reducing production and keeping the original price margins, instead of reducing them and maintaining production levels.

- **Linguistic and cultural differences restrain the movement of human capital.** Apart from top management, which accounts for a mere fraction of total human capital, linguistic and cultural differences are a powerful factor restraining the movement of labor in the single market and introduce another issue of rigidity in human capital among different economic areas. In other words, in the EU system, albeit free, labor does not move as freely as in confederate countries (e.g. the USA, Latin America, the British Commonwealth) that share the same language and, generally speaking, the same culture.

## The Role of the ECB: Price Stability, Centralized Monetary Policy, Incompatibility with Different EU Systems

In this scenario, the European Central Bank (ECB) has a "mission impossible" trying to attain price stability goals with a linear and centralized method within a system of heterogeneous countries, to wit, the Eurozone. Maneuvers that should be applied for countries with strong economic growth (e.g. higher interest rates to restrain speculative bubbles), are the exact opposite of those needed by countries in recession (lower interest rates to support growth, injections of liquidity). The result is that general economic policies are an ineffective compromise for the 19 individual Eurozone countries.

## The Spread as a General Indicator of Economic Performance

These factors of market rigidity, together with the heterogeneity of the basic driver of productivity, link the single market system rigidly to automatic adjustments with the classical supply and demand mechanism. Yet if the exchange rate is completely rigid, the systemic inefficiencies (incapacity to adjust purchasing power to real productivity/economic performance) compared with another Member State will finally converge in a greater deficit, hence public debt, and therefore, be mediated by other economic factors, on the Spread compared to a more virtuous Member State. Debt stock size, together with market expectations of a Member State's capacity to produce wealth and to repay debt, determine a country's Spread. This incorporates all those factors that the market perceives as part of a country's long-term capacity to compete.

The Spread is a general indicator of a country's performance, namely, an indicator that takes into account differences in a country's economic performance, and debt stock that weighs on the productivity of the system itself, compared with other countries. The greater the Spread the less a country's performance, the less the Spread the better a country's performance. In the DL model we take a country's Spread as a general meter of its economic capacity to compete.

## Inefficient Solutions based on Centralized Monetary Expansion: Factors Determining Productive Asymmetry Remain Unchanged

In this scenario, the ECB has instruments which are powerful but ineffective when it comes to resolving this long-term situation. The ECB has much room for maneuver, injecting currency with the classic upside-down approach to preserve the system, but these instruments only cure symptoms, not the causes of systemic ineffectiveness.

Liquidity is pumped into core markets, but the main actors (banks and governments) are slow and inefficient in reallocating liquidity onto underlying real economy.

In other words, the mass of liquidity pumped into the system remains trapped in the circuits upstream of the market, unutilized or badly allocated. It will not change the status quo since no actor has an individual incentive to make a move. Furthermore this liquidity cannot be allocated where it is most needed but is distributed evenly across all Eurozone countries so that it is too much for some, too little for others, and optimum for none of them.

## Germany and Greece: the Impracticality of Automatic Market Regulation

A glaring case of inefficiency in centralized monetary policy is seen when we analyze countries with diametrically different economic conditions, such as Germany and Greece. The former is a large country, with a structured and diversified economic structure, long-term and efficient economic policies that would lead to currency appreciation in a normal monetary adjustment. In Germany performance is mediated by the performance of all other Member States, currency appreciation does not take place in its entirety, but competes with all the other Eurozone economies to determine the exchange rate of the single European currency in relation to other currencies.

On the contrary Greece has a weak national economy and a high debt. The Greek government is trapped in a debt squeeze that is so tight it leaves virtually no room for long-term structural reform. The economic situation is

so depressed that it has unleashed forms of populism, yet these are destined to flounder if they ever come near governing, i.e. in the face of economic realities.

As regards Greece the ECB is strongly resistant to providing more credit to a country that "doesn't deserve it". Buying Greek debt means spreading the cost of the risk over all citizens in the EU. This is difficult to defend, especially when it is obvious that the debt will not be repaid given the basic economic conditions. In this context more concessions in debt purchase are simply a form of unproductive handout and not repayable.

More help will not change the inefficient system, but only mop up emergencies. The country has no capacity to recoup its competitiveness, it does not have the investment capacity to relaunch the national economy, it cannot adjust its own inefficient economy with exchange rates, it cannot engage in downward wage adjustment, nor create inflation with dedicated expansive money policies.

In countries with low productivity, wage rigidity, no exchange rate mechanism and a consequent increase of debt there is virtually no room to maneuver for reform. Centralized reforms are difficult to carry out, unpopular and take time and it is likely that the country does not have the economic and cultural resources to take this step.

Finally, directly helping Greece would create discontent in other countries that had taken mature and virtuous choices involving sacrifices in order to create wealth, and which are now unwilling to cede this to a country that took a non-virtuous path.

# MODELLING THE NEW MONETARY POLICY

In this scenario, we believe that the ECB has the opportunity to pursue a new task. Money supply has to be used not only for traditional price stability policies, but also as an active tool to manage the real economy and to rebalance asymmetries amongst the Member States.
In modelling the DL policy we took into account different perspectives and concepts, as follows.

## A New Role for the ECB: Replacing the Exchange Rate Mechanism Cancelled by the Introduction of the Euro with Monetary Policy Instruments

With inhibited exchange rates and national monetary policies, can we neutralize market rigidity in order to guarantee better economic performance for the entire system? To achieve this, we need to create a monetary mechanism to replace, or "emulate", the adjustment of national currency lost with the introduction of the single currency, and thus to manage localized inflationary pressures within the system. Until this is achieved, market actors work in conditions of rigidity and monetary inefficiency, with consequent economic tension and a probable structural increase of Eurozone total debt in the long-term.

## Natural Selection as a Driver of Systemic Prosperity

With an approach borrowed from evolutionary science the natural selection of businesses is generally the factor that guarantees the greatest economic prosperity for a country in the long run. According to classical economic theory, the maximum liberalism guarantees the maximum expression of natural selection. Economies resistant to change, in which businesses are subsidized or helped artificially, will have lower and slower rates of natural selection and will in turn have a negative effect on the increase of the system's productivity in the long-term. On the contrary, economies where selection is strong and rapid, develop greater productivity and competitiveness in the long run and on global markets. This makes it vital to insert parameters into our model that give the maximum pressure to 'firms selection', in order to obtain the sustainability of the system long-term and prosperity on international markets.

Yet we believe that if market liberalism operates in conditions of rigidity inherent in the economic system, that we can identify an instrument that can release its natural efficiency.

## Maximizing Individual Utility and the Competitive Non-cooperative Game Theory

It is a well-known fact that in a free model the search for an individual's greatest utility does not coincide with a Pareto optimal, and thus with the maximization of the total utility of the system for players. The models where activities are regulated by a framework in which players operate freely according to unbreakable rules, demonstrate that the general and individual utility produced improves. This approach is gaining ground from a practical perspective in the new business models.

We are therefore faced with a typical situation of a theory of competitive non-cooperative games, where players are the States belonging to the Eurozone. Every country, despite solidarity being one of the founding values of the European Union, seeks to maximize its individual interests under the pressure of popular consensus and doing so it unbalance the overall system. For this reason, one of the key principles of Distributed Liquidity is the use of game theory to create a system in which each country, enterprise and citizen, seek its own usefulness, and in doing so improve the system by bringing it to a point of optimum balance.

A proposal that does not take account of this assumption would not be able to have any sustainable results in the long term.

## Macro Trends in Business and Worldwide: from Centralized to Distributive Models

Before considering the merits of the Distributed Liquidity model we must focus on the macro-trend of business organization established since 2005, that is, the *gradual transition from centralized models to distributed models of organization.*

There are many examples across sectors which demonstrate that greater increases of productivity, and hence economic success of businesses, have taken place using this system. Examples include crowdfunding in financing, cloud computing in informatics, e-lancing in work, wikisourcing in culture, networking in communications, bottom-up generation in applications, and microgeneration in energy production.

In all these models the success factor has been to release the energies of innovation, creativity and productivity of single individuals within a regulated schema in which an advantage for an individual becomes an advantage for the community. In this way, thousands of actors seeking their own best interest produce enormous quantities of utility that are released into the community. It is precisely in this context that we witness the best cases of business success which have increased turnover to match the achievements of companies with decades of growth behind them, and in the space of a few years.

One of the basic components of the DL model is this shift in approach from the business world to the world of classical economics, seeking a mathematical solution to transform centralized monetary policies into widespread or distributed policies.

## The Source of the Money Supply: Opening Pandora's Box

Perhaps one of the most courageous and innovative aspects of the DL economic proposal, is printing money. We are aware that the mere mention of this practice could lead to the barricades going up for the entire community of world economists. We are well aware, in fact, that printing money is one of the most dangerous practices in economics; its use and abuse has produced countless instances of hyperinflation and consequent destruction of the economy for decades (even today, as in Venezuela).

Nevertheless, I will show that it is possible to print money and to exclude mathematically the hyperinflation risks. At the same time, we are faced with a totally unconventional approach to the use of issuing money, which opens up new fields of research.

## Helicopter Money, Quantitative Easing and Distributed Liquidity

Distributed Liquidity can be considered as evolution, or rather the solution to be able to apply the concept of Helicopter Money and QE for people.
The limits of the classic version of Helicopter Money are many, and it is true that it has never been applied in practice. However, in conditions of deflation or liquidity trap, it often returns to prominence as an option to be assessed.

This is why HM and QE for people have limitations:

1. They only affect consumption, not investment (if not indirectly)

2. The Prize offered to citizens does not automatically translate as consumption, but is more likely to become savings

3. It was only destined for a simple single-country System and not a complex multi-country system such as the EU.

DL offers a solution that resolves these limitations and makes the concept of distributing money applicable to the bottom basis.

## The Starting Point: Agents of Change

If the greatest challenge for a country in economic difficulty is to recover competitiveness and thus a change its own domestic economic model, the first question is "In an economic system which agents shape economic change most with their choices?"

The reply is very important when it comes to anchoring the Distributed Liquidity model correctly is: Citizens and Businesses. To give the economy the oxygen it needs and to stimulate long-term structural recovery, we need to increase consumption immediately and make greater investments in the medium and long-term.

How can we do this? The response is that each time a citizen exerts their purchasing power and chooses one product rather than another, they are allocating resources to the product perceived as best on the market in terms of its quality/price ratio. In this way they determine the natural selection where virtuous businesses survive and inefficient and obsolete ones do not. Moreover a pick-up in consumption is the first indicator of economic recovery, with its well-known economic effects on orders and production. On the other hand, businesses in search of greater profits search for internal efficiency and the renewal of products to maintain market competitiveness.

These two key factors, *consumption* for citizens and investments for businesses, are the two greatest motors of the economic system, from which all the other parameters follow.

*Citizens*

Traditional policies to stimulate consumption mainly occur by increasing wages or cutting taxes. Yet these instruments are often ineffective, for two reasons:

1. In a depressed system with a high level of uncertainty, the greater availability of resources for the citizen is not transformed into greater consumption, but a crucial part of it takes the form of a greater tendency to save, and this does not produce the desired effect of an economic relaunch.

2. Within the same system increased public wages, or lower taxation of citizens on goods, immediately generates a greater public deficit with a consequent increase in deficit and hence a further deterioration of a country's overall performance in terms of the Spread.

**To obtain the desired effect, greater resources must be linked directly to greater consumption.** Since this is impossible with standard government policies our aim is to provide the agent of change (the citizen) with an incentive only at the precise moment when they bring a utility to the system (to wit, rewarding efficient businesses by buying goods or services, thus increasing consumption) and only if this action really takes place (or by activating a real increase of consumption, with an immediate impact on orders and production for efficient businesses). Thus each unit of currency injected into the system will have maximum effectiveness. Furthermore such major resources will come from outside the system (not national budgetary policy), to avoid any impact on public budgeting.

*Businesses*

We have seen how business culture is a basic driver of a country's competitiveness. This concept includes a range of aspects that have an impact on the productivity of work. These include strategic vision, international capacity, organization of work, R&D, efficient productivity, workforce's attitude to productivity etc. All these factors are extremely difficult to develop autonomously in the short-term and economic or fiscal policy are of little use if they do not change the substratum of the private entrepreneurial and public managerial framework. The goal is to attract agents of change from virtuous countries, not only foreign capital. Primarily the goal is to attract managerial expertise from countries where these qualities are more developed and have brought about concrete and quantifiable results. How can we attract these agents of change with monetary policy in a country in crisis where operating conditions are extremely difficult due to a series of factors?

**As a whole, the concepts embedded in the mathematical formulation of the Distributed Liquidity are:**

- **Free market vs handouts approach in solving economic problems**

- **Application of the theory of competitive non-cooperative games amongst EU member states**

- **Crowd based vs centralized approach to market management**

- **Enhanced Natural Selection of companies for long-term system competitiveness**

- **A Money Issuing system that excludes hyperinflation and offers the solution of Helicopter Money**

- **Identification of the Agents of Change as the starting point to create a virtuous system**

The question is whether we can construct an economic framework in which citizens, businesses and governments can compete and thus generate indirect utility for all actors. Can wealth be created in a heterogeneous market of asymmetric factors and distributed it in a way that is efficient, sustainable and equitable in the long run? In doing so can we create a monetary environment that makes the system sustainable long-term?

The reply lies in the Distributed Liquidity model.

# DISTRIBUTED LIQUIDITY

IN FORMULATING THE DISTRIBUTED LIQUIDITY MODEL WE HAVE SET THE FOLLOWING 6 ECONOMIC OBJECTIVES:

1. Substituting currency exchange with mechanisms having the same final effect on the real economy, while maintaining the single currency.

2. Managing national inflationary/deflationary pressure by compensating it short-term and balancing it long-term

3. Helping countries in short-term crisis and stimulating their return to competitiveness in the mid-term to long-term

4. Rewarding virtuous countries and their citizens, spreading their successful business models to other countries

5. Generating action by agents of change in order to achieve objectives 3 and 4

6. Implementing a model with an automatic and anticyclical mechanism that functions without direct political input and autonomously tends to equilibrium.

# CONCEPTS UNDERLYING
# THE DISTRIBUTED LIQUIDITY (DL) MODEL

1. **The Need for Liquidity and Availability of Liquidity as Two Mutually Exclusive Factors**
   To date, the need for liquidity is decided and negotiated directly by governments on international monetary markets, rather than by the European Central Bank and the International Monetary Fund. Once defined and formalized, this money supply (state bonds, bridging loans, etc.), becomes available to the government concerned, which spends it in line with classical economic policy. DL breaks with this classic schema and the quantity of new currency is not made available to central governments.

2. **Available liquidity is assigned to agents of change.** Once disengaged, the liquidity previously trapped in government and banking circuits can be injected directly and on a broader basis to the agents of change, namely, citizens and businesses, thus freeing up the productive energies of millions of agents rather than just a few hundred institutional Decision Makers.

3. **Among the agents of change DL selects and rewards the most virtuous.** This liquidity is assigned at the base and rewards the most virtuous agents of change. These are: citizens who have made painful political choices in the past and who are now reaping their rewards; and those businesses most able to create added value and wealth.

4. **Binding the rewards to the most virtuous countries to be spent on underperforming countries.** By doing so we achieve a win-win equilibrium: helping the countries in need and at the same time rewarding the virtuous ones.

Taking two countries which are diametrically opposed, Germany and Greece, today Greece needs liquidity since its economy is in trouble, public services are unable to deliver and society is practically in gridlock. This liquidity, contracted with the ECB, goes to the government which "tries" to carry out reforms, but is probably unable to complete them because they are politically unpopular, because it is overwhelmed by emergencies, because it is economically long term, or due to a lack of technical capacity. The result is keeping the status quo, with handouts, a lack of innovation and greater debt at the expense of other Eurozone citizens. Continuing to provide liquidity is simply a handout that maintains the same productive model but without any structural change.

In the Distributed Liquidity model, however, once the Monetary Stimulus needed for Greece has been quantified, it will not go to the Greek government, unable to actuate the change, or to Greek citizens and businesses, with inefficient business models and thus poor economic performance (in aggregate).

In the Distributed Liquidity model the Monetary Stimulus is assigned to citizens and businesses in Germany in the form of a Reward to be used exclusively on Greek territory. This simplified example illustrates how the mechanism works in detail.

# MECHANISMS OF AUTOMATIC ALLOCATION OF DISTRIBUTED LIQUIDITY

These mechanisms are vital in implementing Distributed Liquidity, insofar as they are the motor of the action that we want to induce in the targets of economic monetary policy. Without these mechanisms the DL model is ineffective.

**Mechanisms for Citizens**

- The citizen in a virtuous country (Germany) receives as an automatic Reward a refund equals of VAT for every purchase made on the physical territory of a country in difficulty (Greece)

- The Reward is only for purchases made with electronic currency (credit cards, etc.) and is immediate, taking place at the moment of purchase

- Total Rewards are provided by the ECB as a Monetary Stimulus distributed directly to final beneficiaries and without involving national governments

Let us imagine the concrete application of DL in the real world. For example, a German citizen on Greek territory for work, study or tourism would immediately be credited with 23% of VAT on their credit card for every purchase made on Greek territory. On the one hand, the German citizen has a direct advantage in the tangible and substantial Reward that they earn. On the other hand, purchasing goods and services on Greek territory will increase consumption and thus indirectly develop the entire local economic fabric. Below I present the mathematical formulations and the direct and indirect economic effects of the DL mechanism.

## Mechanisms for Business

- Profits generated by business in virtuous countries (Germany) to a country in crisis (Greece), receive a Reward equal to local taxes on profit.

- Total Rewards distributed are provided by the ECB directly to countries in difficulty at the time of tax payment.

Here the activation of the agent of change occurs based on the first decisional driver of business, i.e. profit maximization. If the generation of profit in an outperforming country for a series of factors, the solution also lies in the automatic mechanism of Rewards to the best firms in the system. Let us imagine, its practical application in Germany and Greece once special regulations clear the international scenario of attempts to exploit indebtedness (carousel fraud, holding companies, etc.).

German business will have a strong stimulus to invest directly in Greece (subsidiaries, new productive plant, acquisitions of businesses with untapped potential, etc.), attracted by the opportunity to earn untaxed profits and to increase shareholder dividends. Here too the Monetary Stimulus is allocated as a Reward to businesses in the virtuous country, and the indirect benefit goes to the country in crisis, which will witness a considerable increase in foreign investments in the short run, but above all, the dissemination of winning business models in its own economic activity in the long run. Here too the impact of this measure is dealt with in the section 'Effects of the Application of the DL Model.'

## Supply/Demand Curve: the Scientific Foundations of Distributed Liquidity

The above implementation mechanisms are the founding basis of the DL and are a guarantee of its effectiveness beyond any other reasonable doubt. In fact, the immediate and contextual repayment of the purchase is to all intents and purposes a reduction in the Price of goods and services.

The Price reduction increases the demand, according to the first law of economics represented by the supply/demand curve.

In the same way, the possibility of having a refund of the tax burden on companies represents a shift in the cost/opportunity curve in favor of the target country.

It follows that the use of the monetary instrument in these terms goes directly to the real economy, producing immediate, tangible and reliable effects, since it is based on the basic assumptions of the economy.

Faced with the powerful and unconventional injection mechanism of Distributed Liquidity based on agents of change, some questions arise.

- In what quantity can these stimuli be given?

- How are stimuli sub-divided among virtuous Member States?

- What impact will stimuli have on inflation in the Member State involved and on its economic system?

- Is this monetary supply resistant to political manipulation?

- What economic and macroeconomic effects can we expect?

Below we define the parameters of the model mathematically, to give it an objective academic and scientific rigor, on which to pursue the analysis of the scenarios and respond to these questions.

## DEFINITIONS

Given a single monetary system X consisting of a group of countries $x$

$x = \{x_1, x_2, ..., x_n\}$

Of which we define following functions, referring to time on an annual basis:

Function of Debt (D):
$$D: X \to R$$
$$X \to R(x)$$

Function of Interest Rates **(R)** on 10-year bonds of countries:

$$R: X \to R$$
$$x \to R(x)$$

Function **Spread (S)** compared to the lowest tax among the countries:
$$S: X \to R$$
$$x \to R(x) - \min_{x \in X} R(x)$$

Function GDP **(GDP)**

$$GDP: X \to R$$
$$x \to GDP(x)$$

# QUANTIFYING THE MONETARY STIMULUS

The quantity of currency injected must be proportional to the size of a country's market and its state of health. Therefore we take Debt as the "Size" of a country's problem and Spread as the "Severity" of the problem faced by that country.

As a consequence the function that determines the Monetary Stimulus (SM) to allocate to every single country x in the economic community is:

$$SM: X \to R$$
$$x \to D(x) \, S(x)$$

This allows us to define the size of total monetary stimulus, SMT of the system X $(SMT_{(x)})$:

$$SMT = \sum_{x \in X} SM_{(x)}$$

## Box 1. Example of application

| MEMBER STATE | GDP IN B€ | PUBLIC DEBT % | TOTAL DEBT | SPREAD | (D)* (S) Quantity of Monetary Stimulus per Member State in billion € |
|---|---|---|---|---|---|
| Germany | € 3.025 | 71% | € 2.148 | 0 | € - |
| France | € 2.183 | 95% | € 2.074 | 0,34 | € 7,05 |
| Italy | € 1.636 | 132 % | € 2.160 | 1,39 | € 30,02 |
| Spain | € 1.081 | 99% | € 1.070 | 1,34 | € 15,30 |
| Greece | € 249 | 176% | € 438 | 7,34 | € 32,17 |

In this chart we make a simulation based on real values (2016) on DL quantification.

Germany, as the most virtuous country (Spread 0) will not receive any help (Debt x Spread 0 = 0). Greece has the highest Spread, but a small economy and absolute Debt Stock, will obtain 32 billion € a year. Italy has large Debt Stock, but a relatively small Spread, will obtain 30 billion € a year of Monetary Stimulus.

Here we can see that money supply is dynamic over time, and adjusts automatically.

We can also understand/present the total size of the monetary policy thus:
[as above]

| Member State | GDP IN B€ | PUBLIC DEBT | TOTAL DEBT | SPREAD | (D)* (S) Quantity of Monetary Stimulus per Member State in billion € |
|---|---|---|---|---|---|
| Germany | € 3.025 | 71% | € 2.148 | 0 | € - |
| France | € 2.183 | 95% | € 2.074 | 0,34 | € 7,05 |
| Italy | € 1.636 | 132% | € 2.160 | 1,39 | € 30,02 |
| Spain | € 1.081 | 99% | € 1.070 | 1,43 | € 15,30 |
| Greece | € 249 | 176% | € 438 | 7,34 | € 32,17 |
| Czech Republic | € 164 | 41% | € 67 | 0,35 | € 0,24 |
| Romania | € 160 | 38% | € 61 | 3,48 | € 2,12 |
| Hungary | € 108 | 75% | € 81 | 3,35 | € 2,71 |
| Slovakia | € 78 | 52% | € 41 | 0,38 | € 0,15 |
| Luxemburgo | € 52 | 21% | € 11 | 0,34 | € 0,04 |
| Bulgaria | € 44 | 26% | € 11 | 2,36 | € 0,27 |
| Croatia | € 43 | 86% | € 37 | 3,46 | € 1,28 |
| Slovenia | €38 | 83% | € 32 | 1,38 | € 0,44 |
| Lithuania | €37 | 42% | € 16 | 0,86 | € 0,13 |
| Latvia | €24 | 36% | € 9 | 0,51 | € 0,04 |
| Cyprus | €17 | 108% | € 18 | 3,99 | € 0,73 |
| Malta | €8 | 63% | € 5 | 1,16 | € 0,06 |
| Tot. European Union | € 14,625 | | € 14,625 | 1,55 | € 140,71 |

Total Distributed Liquidity equals 140 billion € or 1% of EU GDP (in this scenario).
As differences in Spreads decrease, total DL supply is automatically reduced.

# ALLOCATION OF MONETARY STIMULUS

Once the size of the Monetary Stimulus necessary for every country and in its aggregate is defined, we can see how the availability of new currency is allocated among countries x in the system (to be spent on those countries).

To be rewarded meritocratically, the allocation of the new currency must take into account the economic size of the country (GDP), and its performance at the general economic level.

Let us introduce the Function Indicator of Performance or Reverse Spread Pr(x) of every country in the system:

$$\text{Pr}: X \to R$$
$$X \to \max_{x \in X} S - S(x)$$

The rate of Relative Performance is a general indicator expressed by the market on country x's state of health and capacity to compete. The Spread is the best indicator since it incorporates evaluations such as debt, GDP, actual and expected growth, government policies, resources and infrastructure, a country's capacity to prosper, etc. All these are summarized and expressed in percentages of extra Reward, in interest on the Debt as capacity to repay its own debts in the future.

## Box 2. Reverse spread as performance Index

| MEMBER STATE | SPREAD | REVERSE SPREAD- PERFORMANCE INDEX |
|---|---|---|
| Germany | 0 | 7,34 |
| France | 0,34 | 7 |
| Italy | 1,39 | 5,95 |
| Spain | 1,43 | 5,91 |
| Greece | 7,34 | 0 |

In this simplified 5 country chart we see that Greece has the highest Spread of EU: 7.34
The national performance index equals 7.34 – national spread. Italy for example is 7.34 – 1.39 = 5.95

Hence the concept of Reverse Spread indicates overall Performance in terms percentages of country x compared with other countries in the system, i.e. it is the difference between the Spread of the least-well performing country and that of country x.

Let us define the function of Absolute Performance (P) the Relative Performance for the "dimension" of the market expressed in its GDP, or its value in absolute terms:

$$P: X \to R$$
$$x \quad GDP(x) \, Pr(x)$$

Finally, the function of Reward $U(x)$ as the allocation of Monetary Stimulus that country $x_i$ must spend in country $x_j$.

$$P: X \to R$$
$$x \ \text{GDP}(x) \ \text{Pr}(x)$$
$$(xI, xJ) \to \frac{SM(xi) \ P(xj)}{\sum_{x=2} P(Xx)}$$

In sum, this function expresses the quantity in absolute terms of currency made available to every country X in the system to spend in all the other countries in the system.

Each country is awarded a quantity of currency in proportion its economic size (D) and its problems (S). This quantity will be divided in proportion to its economic size (GDP) and performance (Reverse Spread) of every country in the Eurozone.

Furthermore, in resolving the equation the countries themselves (apart from the worst performer) we obtain a stock of available currency. This will be used to apply the policy of DL for the compensation of national economic areas at the regional level (see infra).

## BOX 3: REVERSE SPREAD MULTIPLIED FOR GDP: ABSOLUTE PERFORMANCE INDEX

| MEMBER STATE | SPREAD | REVERSE SPREAD-PERFORMANCE IDEX | (GDP)* (Pr) ÍNDEX PERFORMANCE | % OF MONETARY STIMULUS ON TOTAL |
|---|---|---|---|---|
| Germany | 0 | 7,34 | 22,204 | 23,60% |
| France | 0,34 | 7 | 15,281 | 16,24% |
| Italy | 1,39 | 5,95 | 9,734 | 10,35% |
| Spain | 1,43 | 5,91 | 6,389 | 6,79% |
| Greece | 7,34 | 0 | - | 0,00% |

In this chart we see that relative performance index is multiplied for GDP. The result is an absolute performance index that takes into account the performance and size of a country. The resulting ranking is then converted to percentage. That percentage represents the quota of monetary rewards assigned to a country to be spent in the target country.

For example Germany will be assigned 23% of the 30 billion € destined to Greece.

With this model the Monetary Stimulus is tightly linked to, and directly correlated with, economic stimulus for the development of businesses and increasing consumption. Theoretically, to arrive at a perfect allocation of available resources, its end use, that is, the rewards per consumption Uc and rewards on profits Ui should be,

$$UC + UI = MS$$

In fact, at the moment the model is implemented we can expect a delay in the actions of agents of change, due to information, understanding, planning and the end use of the stimulus. Consequently, in the period of application, only a part of the liquidity is used.

This gives us 2 scenarios:

**1.** $UC + UI < MS$ the unutilized stock goes to a monetary reserve available for subsequent years.

**2.** $Uc + UI > MS$ an excess of requests can be managed in a percentage shared among businesses requiring (greater equity) or on the basis of priority of demand (speed of economic effect).

Other procedural mechanisms can be modelled to maximize the effect on the choices of the agents of change.

## SELF-BALANCING OF THE MODEL LONG-TERM

The use of Distributed Liquidity allows us to activate the conduct of the agents of change and consequently dynamics with powerful macroeconomic implications. We have seen the allocation mechanism of the new currency on the agents of change.

Let us assume that the use of the instrument produces a positive final effect on a country's real economy, defined here as the Efficiency Rate 'a', that is, the capacity that every stock of currency allocated and employed will impact positively on the economy and finance of every country subject to the stimulus.

Consequently we assume that, if the real economy and its microeconomic data are positive, the original Spread will drop by a fraction in the period of time period under review.

$$a: X \to (0;1)$$
$$x1 \to a\ (x_i)$$

So that its effect on the Spread will be, on every country:

$$S(n) = (1-a)^n\ S(0)$$

That is, the state of economic-financial health is reflected in the Spread as a synthetic indicator of market expectations, consequently in the following financial year $t = 1$ the Spread will drop by a fraction of the total at time $t=0$, inversely proportional to the effectiveness of the stimulus, so that:

$$S(t,x_i) = [\ 1 - a(x_i)]^1\ S(0,x_i)$$

In other words, the Stimulus produces improvement in a country which then reduces its Spread. A lower Spread entitles the country to lower

Rewards the following financial year producing a lesser (but still positive) effect, that again reduce the Spread, albeit less rapidly, and so on, defining an asymptotic function tending to zero for every country.

**BOX 4: EFFECTS OF DL (CONSUMPTION, INVESTMENTS) REDUCES THE SPREAD BY 20% A YEAR (EFFICIENCY RATE OF STIMULUS 20% A YEAR). KEEPING GDP AND DEBT CONSTANT, THE TOTAL AMOUNT OF MONEY DECREASES AND TENDS TO 0**

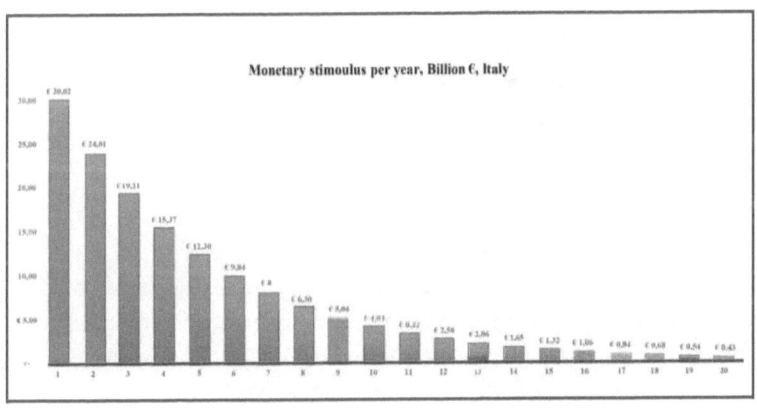

If this is true for a country, the sum of all countries will be the sum of all the functions of all Monetary Stimuli hence:

$$STOT^{(t)} = \sum_{i=1}^{n} s(t, x1)$$

that is

$$STOT^{(t)} = \sum_{i=1}^{n}[1-a(x_1)]t\ S(t, xi)$$

In other words the sum of the Spread variably tending to zero, produces a function of the Spread in aggregate tending to zero. If we express this function as a function of infinite time we obtain:

$$\lim_{t \to +\infty} S_{TOT}(t) = \lim_{t \to +\infty} \sum_{i=1}^{n}[1-a(x_1)]t\, S(t, x_i) = 0$$

Accordingly, if total Spread tends to zero, Total Monetary Stimulus will also progressively tend to zero;

$$SMT(t) = \sum_{x \in X} SM_{(x,t)}$$

$$\lim_{t \to +\infty} SMT(t) = \sum_{i=1}^{n}[D_i] \lim_{t \to +\infty} Si(t) = 0$$

In other words, since the effect of localized Monetary Stimulus is the reduction of the Spread (better economic prospects, no chance to default, an upturn in consumption, and an increase of tax revenues etc.), in the following period the Monetary Stimulus will be a fraction of the original amount.

This fraction will have less impact so that the reduction of the Spread will be less, albeit still present, reducing the Spread and the stimulus tendentially and asymptotically to zero.

But since the Monetary Stimulus is simply the product of the Debt Spread, extending the Spread means that the Monetary Stimulus will also tend to zero. Consequently, if this applies for a country, it also applies for the sum function of all the countries in the system.

Hence we come to the deeper meaning of the application of the DL model:

1. In the long term the model leads levels out the Spread among Member States as an expression of their economic harmonization

2. Therefore the creation of currency to sustain Distributed Liquidity tends to zero over time

3. Consequently the system tends autonomously to equilibrium

The injection of currency is made in a discretional way and not as part of a mathematical model that foresees its equalization, always carries a risk of abuse with consequent hyperinflationary dynamics and economic disintegration.

## Other Considerations

The instrument of Distributed Liquidity functions as a protective shield for single economies and the entire system.

It operates on single economies since the model provides for an automatic intervention in situations of need, exogenous and endogenous. Let us imagine an economic meltdown not due to bad government economic policies but to natural disasters, war, epidemics etc. Without the safety-net of the policy of Distributed Liquidity the Spread would rise immediately and much more drastically, amplifying the effects of the natural disaster. On the contrary, markets reassured by the certainty of a rapid, efficient and automatic intervention of Distributed Liquidity will have a lower perception of the country risk, and thus have a lower increase of the Spread compared to a situation with no such mechanism, thus mitigating the financial effects of the disaster.

It operates within the system giving all economies a basic driver with a centripetal tendency to equalize actors (and not centrifugal, as is currently the case), reassuring markets about the system's persisting grasp, thus creating a belief in its long-term development. This trust is transformed into a reduction of the Spread at the systemic and extra-systemic level, with consequent lower financial costs within the system and greater resources released for development.

Finally, DL do not operates to redistribute wealth from the richest to the poorest: it will help the poorest to reach the richest country of the system.

# CREATION OF THE MONETARY STIMULUS

ISSUING MONEY WITH DISTRIBUTED LIQUIDITY:
NEUTRALIZING RISK OF HYPERINFLATION

Of the various options to create Monetary Stimulus the most suitable instrument is Issuing new Currency.

Traditionally this has been used to finance public spending. Historically, the misuse of this instrument with the uncontrolled printing of money has led to hyperinflation and the destruction of the economic environment. This is why the practice has long since been abandoned in more advanced countries.
The problem of this type of use is that if the increase in the monetary mass does not follow the increase in the economic dimension (real economy), it inevitably dilutes the value of the unit of money, triggering an inflationary spiral with consequences which are well-known to the Economic Community.

Distributed Liquidity allows us to regain this instrument, with a role, functions and a completely new mode of operating. In the DL, the new currency is put into circulation by engaging on one side to consumption (immediate repayment of a share of the electronic payment of an asset), and on the other to the production of value (reimbursement of the tax burden on the profits produced by a company).
In addition, this input of money through real economy via actors outside the domestic economy (foreign international consumers and firms).

In this way the new currency hooks up to the real economy, and is regulated by an automatic mechanism that is automatically reduced up to 0 when economic conditions improve.

We have mathematically demonstrated that the risk of hyperinflation is excluded in this model. On The contrary, it is possible to use this monetary policy to fight deflation, as long as an intervention is necessary.

In situations of deep economic crisis with interest rates approaching zero and with the risk of a liquidity trap, centralized systems to increase the Monetary Base seem unable to combat deflation or inflation close to zero. But with the DL mechanism we can resort to issuing currency not as a mere increase of the Monetary Base in the hands of national governments, but as an active instrument to manage markets, without the fear of hyperinflationary pressure.

With Distributed Liquidity we can inject liquidity exactly where it is needed in order to stimulate inflation and activate the agents of change for economic recovery in countries where the need of currency is greatest and most urgent.

In other words, printing currency, divided up and distributed directly to the Companies and Citizens, being quantitatively proportional to the need of the single country measured with the absolute Reverse Spread, will close the monetary gap in proportion to the size of the problem, stimulating consumption and investment balancing deflationary pressure of countries in crisis and neutralizing the action of the stimulus on the entire system in the medium and long-term.

At this point, the classical instruments and centralized monetary policy come into play again. Faced with a homogeneous and neutral system from the perspective of internal inflationary pressure they could concentrate on international monetary policy to improve the efficiency of the system.

This concept can be seen in the pyramid of monetary instruments:

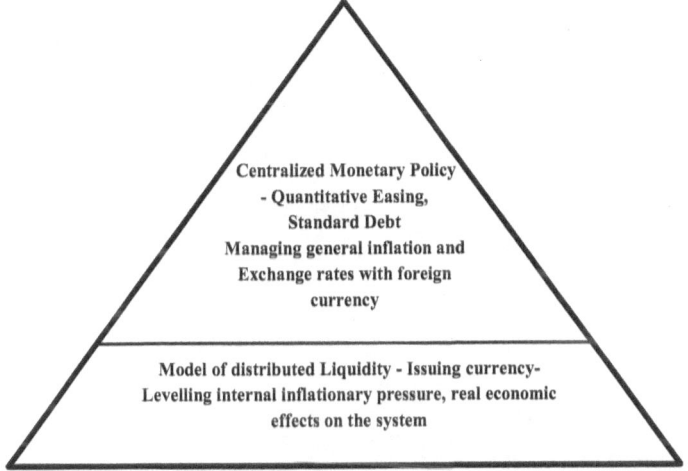

Distributed Liquidity created by Issuing Currency is a way to level out internal localized inflationary dynamics, and to improve economic performance. The resulting economic system, inflationary and homogeneous, would then be governed as a whole with classical centralized monetary policies, based on issuing currency by means of Debt, Quantitative Easing or other instruments, to manage core inflation and the exchange rate with currencies outside the system.

The two instruments are complementary and allow the maximum efficiency and control of the entire monetary system.

From a practical perspective, DL should therefore be regulated by an ECB issuing institution, with the task of managing all digital transactions of re-crediting to level out European and financed by Issuing Currency.

# EFFECTS OF THE APPLICATION OF THE DL MODEL

EXPECTED BEHAVIOR OF AGENTS OF CHANGE: CITIZENS

- **Selective increase in consumer demand in countries receiving Rewards.** From a microeconomic perspective, the immediate and direct savings on the purchase of goods and services equals a decrease in prices and therefore will increase demand in countries most in need of a stimulus for consumption.

- **Effect on immediate consumption.** As the benefit is directly linked to the phase of purchasing goods or services, the effects are immediate at the moment of activation of the DL, anticipating the time and modality of classic injections of liquidity through the banking and government systems.

- **Help for countries in crisis through a direct benefit to one's own country (helping a country in crisis produces a direct benefit for the helper).** From a consumer psychological perspective, for the European citizen the DL incentive system would certainly have an appeal and hence be easy for governments to defend to their electorates. Indeed, we pass from a model of help, purely in handouts (debt purchase or financing countries which are technically undeserving) to a model where help for a country in crisis produces a direct advantage for citizens of more virtuous countries.

- **Sharp increase in human capital mobility in the market.** We are likely to witness a marked increase of human capital exchange within the system. Travel for work, study or tourism will be economically more beneficial and hence will increase the total volume of mobility with a consequent increase in consumption.

- **Social exchange and cohesion among individuals for a more integrated and tolerant Europe.** The increase of an 'international community' within single countries will help to understand, accept and share and would in the end be a powerful driver of integration, based on the increase of individual utility and not on systemic welfareism. An intense exchange in culture, work and social activity is the best driver to reduce nationalist and populist tendencies.

# EXPECTED BEHAVIOR OF THE AGENTS OF CHANGE: FIRMS

- **Immediate pressure to direct investment in the country with available stimuli.** The opportunity of a complete detaxation of profits for business, much like tax havens, is the factor of maximum attraction and stimulus for setting up or acquiring productive activities in less competitive countries.

- **Pressure to generate maximum profits.** The opportunity to obtain an advantage on profits without the fear of excessive taxation and in a perfectly legal way, would push businesses, productive activities and financial holding companies to release the maximum possible profits rather than hiding them behind budgetary policies designed to minimize profits and lessen fiscal impact (if not to divert them altogether).

- **Consequent implementation of efficient and effective systems of business management.** Generating profits is the final indicator of businesses' utility-generating capacity. This is the fruit of virtuous practices on all company levels: financial management, human resource management, management of productive processes, marketing and international trading systems, research and applied development, etc. These virtuous practices are the basis to create a living productive environment and to prosper in the long run, thus creating a powerful driver for its Spread vs. the natural rigidity of organizations when it comes to change.

- **Mergers and Acquisitions (M&A) on businesses in countries in crisis and the internationalization of business.** In addition to the creation and transfer of new productive activity of virtuous countries to the less virtuous, there would be a natural tendency towards M&A on national firms with poor production, but high growth potential.

At the operational level, M&A means the introduction of virtuous practices of business management, with a change of business culture which is normally difficult and slow without the injection of outside expertise.

- **Transmission of expertise on the territory of countries in crisis.** Once introduced in large national companies this expertise and culture will spread to the productive environment upside-down way. Large companies working with local sub-contractors demanding productive and qualitative standards will press local SMEs to adapt and hence to change their own production models positively, generating an effect of improvement widespread of a company's management capacity.

- **Cultural trans-European diffusion of virtuous models of business management.** This mechanism leads to a powerful acceleration in transferring high-productivity practices by more efficient countries to less efficient countries. In the long run this creates a mechanism of increased competitiveness not only of more economically backward countries, but also of the entire system. This means an economic base multiplier that would speed up the entire system in terms of economic progress, and thus greater competitivity long-term. Systems without this incentive mechanism cannot act in a comparable way.

- **Development of the culture of internationalization in Eurozone SMEs.** Starting internationalization in one EU country is the perfect preparation for small and medium-sized enterprises (SMEs) operating exclusively in the national context. Once the first operation of internationalization has been carried out successfully, businesses will develop a culture of internationalization and the expertise can also be utilized outside the national system. A company preparing to take part in international activities for the first time in a country within the system develops capacity that it can re-use outside the system. The European system thus becomes a training camp for internationalization, whose costs are compensated by the Monetary Stimulus so as to prepare companies for internationalization outside the EU system.

- **Attraction for Foreign Firms.** The enhanced performance of business in terms of shareholder dividends (for tax cuts and budgetary policy pro utile), will attract more capital and businesses outside the system to invest in countries within the system. In other words, the convenience offered is similar to a tax haven, together with a guarantee of security and protection of the Eurozone system, it is likely to stimulate a return of capital currently parked outside the EU system, in addition to a large flow of extra EU industrial and institutional investors.

## EFFECTS ON THE ECONOMIC SYSTEM

- **Permanent acceleration of Eurozone economic exchanges.** The strong incentives to operate beyond national confines would immediately increase all exchanges among countries in the monetary system, in variable forms, but permanently over time.

- **Acceleration of forms of natural selection in business.** In a market where the closure of old and inefficient firms is stepped up and we witness the birth of new more efficient and competitive groups with M&A, the process of natural selection of firms is accelerated with a more rapid rate of economic renewal even in economic areas which are stagnant and closed to renewal.

- **Consequent improvement of overall systemic productivity in the long and very long term.** In the very long term this creates a powerful multiplier for economic development. An acceleration of the process of natural selection of firms would be proportional to the acceleration of economic growth in general.

- **Greater delocalization of production within the EU Member States, and not extra-EU.** Attracted by favorable tax conditions, business can delocalize productive plant to countries in the system rather than outside it, increasing the economic driving force and limiting the flight of capital and resources.

- **Transnational hybridization of businesses as a motor of the increase of mobility of capital and work in the single market.** Acquisitions, mergers and delocalization would lead to a continuous hybridization of experience, competences and expertise between one Member State and another. These advantages along with a general acceleration of the system and greater "natural selection" in business, will become the pillar of structural economic development over time.

- **Re-entry of capital immobilized or stored in tax havens outside the system.** Give the same advantages as tax havens with greater guarantees and security within a safer, more stable and guaranteed system. This is a strong incentive for the re-entry of capital in countries subject to the Monetary Stimulus. Re-entry of such flows could alone attract large sums of capital which are currently outside the EU system.

- **Immediate reversibility of hybridization.** The injection of Distributed Liquidity can be interrupted at any time and the status quo ante restored without damaging the system and keeping the benefits acquired.

# EFFECTS ON NATIONAL GOVERNMENTS

## Governments in debt

- **DL as a program for international investments attraction.** For countries that require economic relaunch, DL works exactly in the same way on national programs to attract foreign investments, without the relative cost on national budget.

- **Fiscal emergence and the increase of income from direct consumption taxation.** A similar, if not more virtuous, mechanism is the direct consumption of those extranational citizens entitled to a Reward on the territory. In this case, as payment of VAT is directly reimbursed to the citizen digitally and thus traceable by banking movements. The Monetary Stimulus is traceable and will thus generate 100% taxation. This has a powerful and immediate impact on economic microactivities (services, commerce, tourism, property, etc.) where extranational citizens demand digital invoicing and payment. It is in everyone's best interest not to evade taxation: extranational citizens for the direct advantage of reimbursed VAT, and SMEs for the opportunity to tap into a vast public of new foreign clients. This mechanism has a further cultural effect, namely the emergence of total evaders, the minimum business structuring of micro-firms, and a greater propensity to pay taxes by entrepreneurs.

- **Increase of tax revenues from profits of foreign firms.** For less virtuous governments with state revenues permanently in deficit, an increase of new productive activities would mean an increase of revenue from taxation of profits generated by foreign firms. The stimulation of fiscal policy pro utile, thus leads to an immediate effect of greater cash-flow from taxes and hence an improvement in the state budget.

- **Expansion of economic activities and consequent income from other forms of taxation (wages, direct consumption).** The increase in productive activity by foreign companies not only produces direct benefits from taxation on profits, but also benefits from the general expansion of economy on national territory. Greater productive activity means greater income from wage taxation, higher wages mean higher spending and greater revenue from indirect taxation. Likewise, the entire chain of sub-contractors of businesses to foreign business with its greater productive motor, will lead to an upgrade of economic conditions and hence to a greater capacity to pay taxes for local business.

- **Increasing employment.** One direct effect of greater ex-Eurozone investment and increased consumption on the territory, is greater job creation. More employment means greater spending power for citizens released on the territory in the form of consumption. This will initiate a very extensive virtuous process downstream, increasing the redistribution of the resources employed. Moreover, the acceptance of this incentive system by a country wishing to participate is a powerful argument of internal policy.

- **Freedom of economic policy.** Any lack of reform is compensated by a constant process of hybridization from more efficient countries to less efficient countries. The mechanism of Distributed Liquidity can act in synergy and alongside other mechanisms of change through national economic policies. Indeed while the indications of structural reform recommended to countries in crisis by the ECB, IMF and EU remain valid, in cases where it is not possible to realize such reforms due, for example, to a lack of internal political consensus, there is still an automatic balancing mechanism. Help would no longer (or not only) be provided through monetary handouts, but through Distributed Liquidity and thus via bottom-up growth. In short, governments would not necessarily be forced to apply European directives, but they would have to accept an increased presence of foreign firms in sectors of their own national economy.

In any case the trend can be arrested and inverted as the mechanism is automatic, as soon as the adoption of structural reforms to invert the trend are fully effective.

- Pressure from below to reform. If governments fail to apply structural reform, in the long term the spread of new business models designed to generate systemic efficiency, with a greater the presence of foreign firms, and hence economic influence on local lobbies, will create a stimulus from below (firms) to reform the county's bureaucratic and administrative procedures, suggesting more efficient models already tried and tested in other countries.

## Governments with a Budget Surplus

- **DL as a program for the internationalization of companies.** For countries with a strong domestic economy, DL works exactly in the same way on national programs to incentive internationalization, without the relative cost on national budget.

- **Return of untaxed profits for new investment.** In hindsight holding firms will experience a direct benefit in the return of tax-free capital, with the property enrichment of firms and larger dividends for shareholders. This fresh capital would be free for new national and international investment, and thus new economic activity under the control of firms in virtuous countries.

- **Internationalization of national business environment.** The direct consequence is the growth of national businesses based on international development models followed by a flourishing of multinationals based on national headquarters. This means a qualified workforce engaged in activity with a high added value. The shift towards the internationalization of a firm's business environment within the system will also impact on an international level outside the system.

- **Increased company size.** This encourages the growth of firms which will be stimulated to grow in size and to overhaul their management processes in an international perspective in preparation for international development. To face the challenges better, the attraction of making profits tax-exempt means it is likely to see national processes of M&A, with consequent increases in firm size. This is a necessary condition for international competitivity and to combat 'business dwarfism' still present in Europe.

- **Increased mobility of underemployed human capital** (management, technicians, etc.). In this way, high-level human capital of virtuous countries can be used in M&A, delocalization and the management of business in less virtuous countries, to increase employment in virtuous countries and to create a strong incentive to boost mobility for entrepreneurs and managers and hence to the transfer and hybridization of expertise on the territory of the system.

- **High-level employment.** The activity of management of M&A, and consequent activity of operational restructuring calls for high-quality business skills. This leads to an increase in demand for highly qualified, highly skilled figures, thus improving the quality and average pay in the virtuous country.

- **Freedom to experiment economic policies of governments with an automatic safety-net.** In a system where the poor economic performance is immediately compensated by an automatic stimulus mechanism, governments are free to experiment with unconventional domestic economic policies. In the case of failure, there is no risk of systemic contamination, since the intervention of the monetary mechanism acts as a safety-net for the country at least as regards the economic shock to supply and demand, from the perspective of a financial holding for market expectations and relative Spread. This will be a new paradigm: a market, a currency and a single central bank, and freedom of governments to express their own national economic and fiscal policies without the risk of a systemic imbalance.

- **Economic-political influence on the countries most exposed.** A virtuous country, following the 'economic colonization' of non-virtuous countries, will experience an increase in the presence of company decision-makers in key roles in national industries. This means a greater capacity to influence government's economic choices via the activity of institutional industrial representation.

## EUROPEAN GOVERNMENT AND THE EUROPEAN CENTRAL BANK

- **Positive image for the European Union institutions and the ECB.** These will have a financial role vis-à-vis the activities of businesses and private individuals. Thus we can expect a diametrical change in the perception of the ECB and the EU: from distant bureaucratic bodies far from the citizen, to champions of consumers, business and governments in difficulty.

- **Competition among states in realizing virtuous models to obtain greater Monetary Rewards.** The opportunity to access a greater stock of Monetary Stimulus to spend on national companies and citizens is an incentive for governments to realize ambitious economic reforms, in competition with governments of other Member States.

- **Entry of new members in the Eurozone.** If a new country wants to join the Eurozone, the Distributed Liquidity model provides excellent support by means of swift monetary expansion and activation of the agents of change, with immediate effect during the first years of entry. Existing Eurozone countries will find new available liquidity (not detracted for other uses) to stimulate economic activity with that country, and the new entrant will witness a steady flow of investment in its economic fabric and an increase in consumption, as described above.

## MACROECONOMIC AND MONETARY EFFECTS

- **The emulation of effects of exchange rates on the national currency through monetary policy.** In the DL model the recovery of competitiveness would no longer occur through the devaluation of national currency, but through the selective injection of currency (through consumption and investment) to countries in economic-financial crisis. The greater the difficulty (unexpressed currency devaluation), the greater the available liquidity for Member States in need, and the greater the Reward for other countries in the system willing to purchase and invest in that country.

- **Dynamic and automatic adjustment of the model over time and systemic stabilization.** One of our objectives in studying the monetary model is to obtain an automatic anticyclical mechanism independent of day-to-day monetary management. This guarantees a new paradigm of monetary stabilization in the very long term, namely, certainty for markets in which to make long-term evaluations. The Monetary Stimulus injected tends to develop the economic system, making it more competitive and efficient. Over time, the microeconomic effects of this distributed monetary injection in a country in crisis will have a powerful positive effect on the structural improvement of public accounts (see Effects on Businesses and Governments). Consequently the financial markets, now reassured by an automatic (and hence predictable) policy for economic and financial improvement, will enjoy greater security and hence greater trust in purchasing state bonds. The result will be a rapid drop in the Spread of the country in question. In the following financial year less resources will be available for rewards, until theoretically this drops to zero, or when the country becomes the most virtuous country in the system, or when differences among the countries disappear.

Adjustments would thus be gradual until reaching a new point of equilibrium among all players on future prospects and the trend towards a reduction of the Spread by selling off debt stock.

- **Protection from political and governmental influence.** Monetary Stimulus is directly proportional to the lower productivity of the country and to the gap on the Spread caused by debt stock. This means equity in resource allocation and without any political intervention. The advantage of an anticyclical system which is predictable and fixed over time is that it protects the ECB from current tensions and governmental attempts to wield influence, driven by the need for national consensus. As the quantity of stimulus is directly proportional to the need expressed by the market, there would be no need to negotiate every installment of help for countries in difficulty as this would automatically be allocated in an impartial way.

- **Short-term effectiveness (greater consumption by non-Eurozone citizens).** The impact of DL on consumption will be instantaneous, giving immediate respite in critical situations of demand shock. Successively, thanks to the automatic adjustment, the quantity of incentives will be in proportion to the country's actual needs. The deeper the country is in crisis the more Reward resources are freed up and earmarked for virtuous countries to be spent in the country receiving the monetary stimulus. The rapidity is in proportion to the urgency of the economic-financial situation of the receiving country.

- **Medium-to-long term effects (investment by foreign firms).** Similarly, as the model is predictable, virtuous countries would have a greater stock of Rewards earmarked for companies economically active in the country requiring help, with a period of readjustment lasting 5-10 years, sufficient for decisions on delocalization or investment.

- **Maximum efficiency in results.** As the stimuli are exclusively linked to purchasing goods and services made with electronic currency and to firms' profits, their effectiveness is 100% of the total money supply injected. The same liquidity, injected with traditional channels by centralized monetary policies, would be less effective and take much longer to transmit to the real economy.

- **The inflationary pressure of greater investment and consumption in less virtuous countries compensates proportionally the deflationary pressure of a poorly-functioning national economy.** One of the concepts underlying Distributed Liquidity is that if we cannot reduce prices and wages in a country in difficulty due to systemic rigidity (no exchange rate, no opportunity to act on the National Monetary Base), we can balance the system by halting deflationary phenomena in countries in crisis or raise prices by means of moderate inflation in more virtuous countries. As we saw initially countries with a high Spread, namely, those with a strongly negative economic situation due to low productivity and high debt, will experience a downward adjustment for wages and prices in a perfectly elastic market. Since we know that the decline in wages and consumer prices is more rigid than its upturn we will need to stabilize the system, supporting depressed consumption to give an inflationary counterthrust, and to raise prices and wages of other countries in the same system, leaving those of the country subject to allocation unchanged. An injection of Distributed Liquidity, either on consumption or business investment, will create a push not on the basis of handouts, but on activity designed to generate real economy. A country receiving a Reward will enjoy greater financial availability of revenue for its own agents of change (citizens and business). This will allow greater availability of expenditure and hence an increase in national consumption, with a consequent shift to greater inflation in the virtuous country compared to the average for other Eurozone countries.

- **Complementarity of the instrument with other centralized monetary policies.** The injection of selective Distributed Liquidity for countries in greatest need tends to level out inflation among the different areas until reaching a neutral position compared to inflationary pressure of the system as a whole. From here we can re-utilize centralized monetary policies to manage the general inflation rate once cleared of internal inflationary pressure.

- **Application of the model at a regional level.** The Distributed Liquidity model was conceived to resolve problems in the Eurozone but it is also valid in all monetary systems with strong imbalances across areas or regions and that need instruments to even them out. Let us take Italy, for example, a country with strong economic imbalances between regions (Italy, North and South). Traditional policies call for enormous resources in public spending and tax cuts to kick-start the economy. Let us imagine those same resources, no longer used as handouts and inefficient public expenditure, but channeled by the instrument of Distributed Liquidity. On the one hand, this will immediately generate an increase in demand for goods and services. On the other hand, it will make it convenient for entrepreneurs in the North to invest in the South, creating healthy businesses, producing profits and obtaining tax-free profits. Here too, it is not hard to imagine the effect on the real economy with thousands of agents of change immediately stimulated to seek their own individual best interest, and in so doing giving a strong impulse to economic growth for the regions in crisis.

  In the same way the DL model can also be applied to supranational systems that do not share the same currency, provided there is an organism with strong monetary power (e.g. the IMF) that manages implementation. This would open up scenarios of global development not imaginable today.

## CONCLUSION

More than a decade after the introduction of the single European currency, it clear that the simple mechanism of adjusting supply and demand backed by national economic policies cannot compensate for the absence of exchange rates between currencies and monetary autonomy and obtain the homogenization of heterogeneous European economies.

Differences in size, culture, language and the configuration of the economy make it difficult to regulate monetary policy with centralized monetary instruments. These create extreme rigidity in the automatic adjustment of supply and demand, and create inefficiency, reducing purchasing power and as a result fosters discontent among citizens, the business community and Member State governments.

In addition to traditional monetary instruments the introduction of Distributed Liquidity policy will allow Member States to maintain the single currency with its recognized advantages, together with the capacity to balance internal dynamics, neutralize localized deflationary pressure, and to accelerate economic development of the system as a whole, using a model which is equitable, predictable, sustainable, anticyclical, complementary, meritocratic, unifying and ethical.

# ETHICAL CONSIDERATIONS IN APPLYING THE DL MODEL

Beyond its purely economic aspects, the Distributed Liquidity model opens a new era in the process of union and harmony among nations. When individual interest also benefits the interest of others, social relations are more likely to flourish. By contrast, when a foreigner is perceived as a threat to individual interests, anthropologically speaking what we get is hostile and protectionist behavior. DL leads to a constant European melting pot, in which the hosts and those hosted in other countries both have a direct advantage so that living together peacefully is in their own best mutual interest. DL is the social glue binding together the entire economic community that adopts it.

In addition to encouraging cultural exchange among Europeans, DL has another important impact. The system tends to bring countries closer together economically, and thus levels out income differences among citizens of different countries in the long term. In doing so DL creates wealth in the short run for all those contributing to the process, citizens and businesses alike. Harmonizing economies and incomes means taking a first step towards reducing social differences and seeking widespread prosperity for all citizens.

Let us imagine this mechanism implemented globally. There will be a very strong impulse by industrialized countries to invest in developing countries in search of enormous quantities of currency available for making tax-free profits. Developing countries will see a strong flow of foreign investment, and therefore a recovery in local employment. With time, the labor market will be re-structured, social guarantees will increase in parallel with the increase of individual income, and the entire local economy will pick-up.

We should witness a move towards realizing infrastructure and the establishment of educational programs, and in the last instance the activation of a process to obtain widespread prosperity. In the long run the Distributed Liquidity model allows a world economy with lower disparities, greater harmony, more widespread equality, prosperity and with individual interest always ready to act as a vigilant guarantor of the system's equilibrium.

# ADDENDUM
## NEW FIELDS OF RESEARCH

The DL model opens up vast areas for new and original economic research. Here we have singled out some themes for future research, in order to give the model a greater level of detail and forecasting capacity.

1. The scientific basis of DL is the supply & demand curve of basic microeconomics. The injection of liquidity coupled with the moment of purchase is equivalent to reducing prices; consequently we obtain an increase in quantity. Simulating the variation of supply & demand in different Member States and in the aggregate for businesses and citizens as a variation of purchasing and investment behavior in the wake of DL. Tracing the subsequent macroeconomic trends for countries in the system.

2. Distributed Liquidity and Currency Issuance: Effects on localized inflation and overall inflation. The increase of the monetary base injected locally offsets deflationary pressure. The quantity of currency injected is proportional to the size of the Deficit of economic performance and thus proportional to expressed or latent deflation. The increase of the monetary base with selective injections of DL has a neutral impact on general inflation. Draw the new function of general inflation based on the effects of Distributed Liquidity.

3. Split-off of effectiveness factor a. This factor expresses the reduction of the Spread from one year to another. To simplify things it is taken as a constant factor. The effectiveness of the instrument varies with the quantity of Rewards actually used by countries vis-à-vis the country in crisis. Consequently, for every financial year, each country has an efficiency factor $a_x$.

Factor a is the average weight of all factors ax for each country in the system. Formalize the function of the effectiveness factor, correlate the different output with DL estimates and produce forecasts based on the main economic indicators.

4. Comparison of performance of interventions to support the real economy. The performance of a given incentive can be expressed by its efficiency, i.e. the total quantity of currency employed compared to the fraction that actually arrives in the real economy, and its effectiveness, measured by the result in real economy produced. Simulate traditional systems compared to the DL and formalize benchmark indicators.

5. Application of Distributed Liquidity model to the regional and intra-national levels. Simulate the impact of applying DL on the basis of regional macroeconomic indicators and produce forecasts on the effects in the medium-to-long term.

6. Develop a long-term simulation of the application of DL model at the global level in which: Scenario 1 – the Euro expands thanks to Distributed Liquidity in other countries until reaching currency hegemony; and Scenario 2 – Creation of a world currency, the IMF becomes the monetary authority and issuing body for DL worldwide. Implications for global economic harmonization.

# SIMULATED APPLICATION OF DISTRIBUTED LIQUIDITY

This link http://l2l.it/DL1 contains the simulation tables for the application of the Distributed Liquidity model to the countries of the Euro Area (with the addition of the United Kingdom, to highlight the potential benefits if it chose to adopt the single European currency). The data are indicative and the tables give a quantitative idea of Monetary Stimuli that the DL mechanism could generate for each country.

**http://l2l.it/DL1**

## COMMENT ON THE SIMULATION TABLES FOR THE DL MODEL

**Table 1:** This reports the basic indicators GDP, Public Debt and Spread. Through the product of Debt by Spread we obtain the quantification of the Monetary Stimulus needed for each country. The correlation of GDP by Reverse Spread determines the index of absolute performance and hence the percentage of allocation of Rewards on the total.

**Table 2:** Total Monetary Stimulus (TMS) for each country in Table 1 is sub-divided among all countries on the basis of the percentage allocation of the total. Thus, every country obtains Rewards to use in other countries, and every country receives Investment from the other countries on itself.

**Note 1:** The model shows how the most virtuous country in the system, and hence the most economically prosperous, does not receive investment from other countries (they don't need it!). At the same time, having the best Reverse Spread a country receives more Rewards to spend in other countries and thus more capacity to spread its own winning business model for every unit of GDP.

By contrast, the worst-performing country will not have a Reward to spend in other countries (it is unable to transmit winning models), but it will have the maximum Monetary Stimulus made in proportion to its Debt so that other countries come to invest in it.

Note 2: The allocation of Monetary Stimulus highlights that countries also receive a stock of Monetary Stimulus. This is the quantity of currency available to apply Distributed Liquidity at the regional level.

**Table 3:** This simulates the progress of the creation and injection of Monetary Stimulus for Italy keeping all other factors constant. Assuming that the impact of direct foreign investment and consumption in Italy produces an economic up-turn and consequently a reduction of the average annual Spread of 20%, the table shows the trend of aggregate monetary expansion for Italy in the last 20 years.

The effectiveness of the stimulus varies from year to year, but over time it tends to reduce the overall stimulus. Any exogenous shock that suddenly increases the Spread (war, famine, earthquakes, etc.) will produce a short-lived peak before dropping again.

# BIBLIOGRAPHY

It is difficult to cite precise sources used unless I refer to the literally thousands of newspaper articles, journals, academic books, web pages, forum and discussions, television debates, conferences, meetings and conversations over a period of 20 years' academic and professional experience. A mass of unrecorded and unorganized information that began to take shape in 2015, and which has finally crystallized in this publication. Nevertheless, I feel it a duty to cite some sources, even if these do not deal with monetary economics stricto sensu but which have instead helped me develop an unconventional approach to econometric problem-solving and which have sharpened my capacity to get the "big picture" strategically speaking, and not just by using the traditional analytical instruments of classical economics.

A monetary history of the United States 1867-1960 (1971)
Friedman Milton, Schwartz Anna Jacobson

Animal Spirits (2010) - George A. Akerlof

Dal baratto all'euro. Storia della moneta dalle origini ai giorni nostri (2003)
Emanuela Ercolani

Economia dell'unione monetaria (2000) - Paul De Grauwe

Flatlandia (1884) - Edwin A. Abbott

Foundations of International Macroeconomics (1996)
Maurice Obstfeld, Kenneth S. Rogoff

General theory of employment, interest and money (1936)
John Maynard Keynes

Giochi non cooperativi e altri scritti (2004)
John Nash, H. W. Kuhn, S. Nasar

International Economics: Theory and Policy (2005)
Paul R. Krugman, Maurice Obstfeld

Keynes John Maynard: Teoria generale dell'occupazione, dell'interesse e della moneta, e altri scritti (2013) - Alberto Campolongo

La buona moneta: come azzerare il debito pubblico e vivere felici (2018)
Pierangelo Dacrema

Money (1922) - Dennis Robertson

Money and Inflation: A Monetarist Approach (1982)
J. Huston McCulloch

Money and the Mechanism of Exchange (1875)
William Stanley Jevons

Rapporto sull'Unione economica e monetaria nella Comunità europea (1989) - Comitato Delors

Strategic Market Management (1998) - David A. Aaker, Christine Moorman

The Competitive Advantage of Nations (1990) - Michael E. Porter

The Laffer Curve: past, present, and future (2004) - Arthur B. Laffer

The New Classical Macroeconomics (1988) - Kevin Hoover

The optimum quantity of money (1969)
Milton Friedman

The Theory of Interest (1930) - Irving Fisher

The Theory of Money (1978) - Jürg Niehans

The Theory of Money and Credit (1934) - Ludwig von Mises

*«We are continually faced with a series of great opportunities
brilliantly disguised as insoluble problems.»*

*John William Gardner*

If you are an economist interested in developing the arguments dealt with in this essay or the Distributed Liquidity model visit our website:

**www.distributedliquidity.eu**

or write to us at

**info@distributedliquidity.eu**

www.ingramcontent.com/pod-product-compliance
Lightning Source LLC
Chambersburg PA
CBHW030729180526
45157CB00008BA/3102